JUST LOOKING

by

John Allan

Beginnings Series

Series editor: Jim Belben

BIBLE SOCIETY
Stonehill Green, Westlea, Swindon SN5 7DG, England

BRITISH YOUTH FOR CHRIST
Cleobury Place, Cleobury Mortimer, Kidderminster, Worcs. DY14 8JG, England

Photographs
Cover and page 4–ZEFA Picture Library
Page 6–The National Gallery
Page 10–Creative Publishing
Page 12–Camera Press
Page 16–United Bible Societies

First published 1987
Reprinted 1989, 1991

British Library Cataloguing in Publication Data

Allan, John, *1950–*
Just looking: your chance to believe
it or not.–(Beginnings; 1)
1. Christianity
I. Title II. Series
202'.4055 BR125

ISBN 0 564 03144 5
Printed in Great Britain by Stanley L Hunt (Printers) Ltd, Rushden, Northants
Design/Illustration by Rob Pengilley and Richard Deverell

Bible Societies exist to provide resources for Bible distribution and use. Bible Society in England and Wales (BFBS) is a member of the United Bible Societies, an international partnership working in over 180 countries. Their common aim is to reach all people with the Bible, or some part of it, in a language they can understand and at a price they can afford. Parts of the Bible have now been translated into approximately 1,800 languages. Bible Societies aim to help every church at every point where it uses the Bible. You are invited to share in this work by your prayers and gifts. The Bible Society in your country will be very happy to provide details of its activity.

CONTENTS

HOW TO USE THIS BOOK . . .

. . group members

ust Looking is a way of finding out for ourself what Christians really believe, nd whether it makes sense.

We've subtitled this course "your hance to believe it — or not", because ne decisions you reach in this course vill be your **own**. Nobody will be ashing you over the head with a Bible, rying to get you converted in thirty econds in order to set a new world ecord.

We guarantee that three things won't appen. There will be **no mbarrassment**. Nobody is suddenly oing to suggest singing a hymn, or ask ou to pray, or whatever. You won't ave to struggle to keep a straight face vhile weird religious ceremonies are erformed around you.

And there will be **no boredom**. This ourse is easy to understand. You won't nd yourself sitting there with glazed yes, listening politely to a vicar vittering on for ever and ever, while you radually sink into a coma. You **will** nd yourself arguing heatedly, laughing ncontrollably, listening open-mouthed o ideas you have never heard before. If ou don't, complain.

Finally, there will be **no pressure**. You each your own decisions at your own peed, and nobody's going to cry if at ne end of the day your opinions are ifferent from ours. But you **might** just nake the most earth-shattering iscovery of your life.

Try to be at every session — because very bit counts. And especially keep ee the extra Sunday later in the course hen you will be checking out a church nd tucking into a good feed.

If you do all that we suggest, you'll nd — as loads of people have already — nat **Just Looking** can be a lot of fun. nd you might just find something nuch more important, too. So brace ourself. It's going to be an interesting de.

. . . group leaders

The detailed notes for running a **Just Looking** group begin on Leaders' notes page 1 — the tinted pages at the centre of the book.

SESSION

1

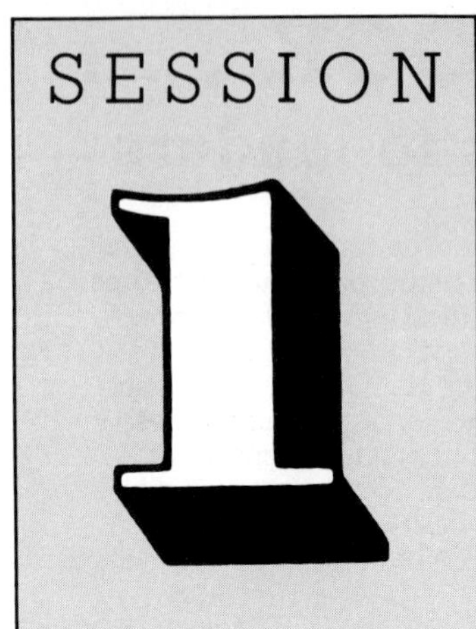

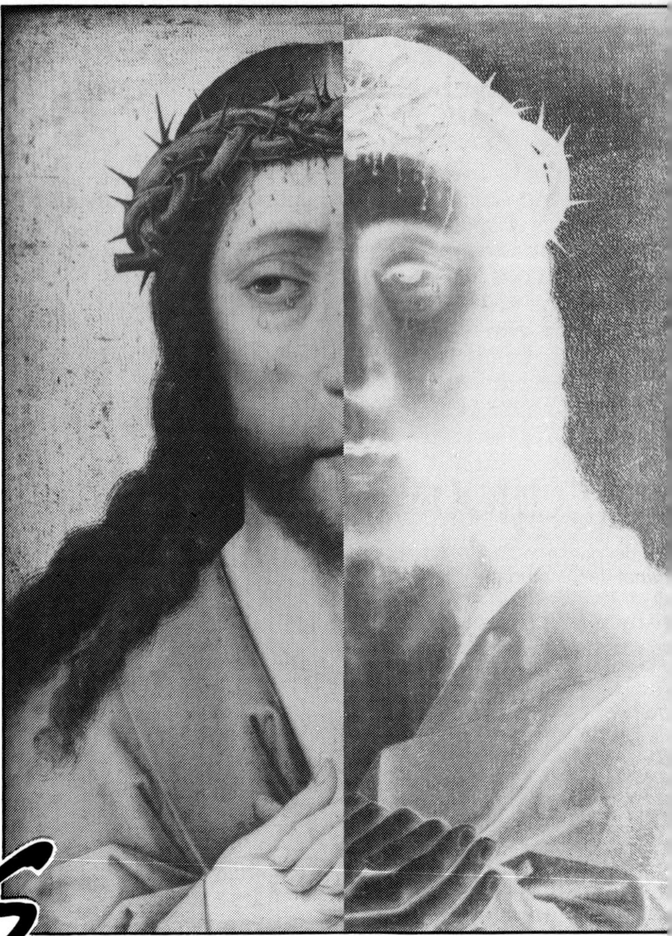

JESUS WHO WAS HE?

STARTER

THE JESUS REPORT

Fill in your answers here . . .

1

2

3

4

5

6

BIBLE DATA

heck out what Jesus had to say about himself. Read through John 12.44–50.

44Jesus said in a loud voice, "Whoever
elieves in me believes not only in me but
so in him who sent me. 45Whoever sees me
es also him who sent me. 46I have come
to the world as light, so that everyone who
elieves in me should not remain in the
arkness. 47If anyone hears my message and
oes not obey it, I will not judge him. I came,
ot to judge the world, but to save it.
48Whoever rejects me and does not accept
my message has one who will judge him. The
words I have spoken will be his judge on the
last day! 49This is true, because I have not
spoken on my own authority, but the Father
who sent me has commanded me what I
must say and speak. 50And I know that his
command brings eternal life. What I say,
then, is what the Father has told me to say."
(John 12.44–50)

BACKGROUND

Is this passage a fair reflection what Jesus taught?

It used to be thought that the ospel of John was written enturies after Jesus had lived, someone who knew very little the facts or the background. ow we know this is not true.

It is believed that the Gospel as written within seventy naybe even forty) years of sus' death. Many eyewitnesses no could have challenged any tional additions, were still alive.

Archaeological finds have own that the author knew erusalem as it was in Jesus' ay.

"Father" was a name Jesus ten used for God. The famous ord's Prayer" calls God ather."

REACTIONS

1. **Are there any things you don't understand about this passage, and would like explained?**
2. **What did Jesus say he had come into the world to do?**
3. **Where did Jesus claim his ideas came from? Do you think this is a bit arrogant?**
4. **What did Jesus say would happen to those who believed and obeyed him?**
5. **Would Jesus have agreed with this description of himself? Why / Why not?**
6. **Is there anything else in this passage you want to discuss before moving on?**

7 | 8 | 9

ASK YOURSELVES...

? **How did you find out what you know about Jesus?**

BACK-UP DATA

Some more Bible passages to explore:

- What did some of the earliest disciples believe about Jesus? See an example in Philippians 2.6–11.
- What did Jesus believe about himself? See what he said in Mark 14.53–62.
- What impression did Jesus make on ordinary people? See what they said in Matthew 7.28–29.

FACT-FILE

■ Do other writers of the time mention Jesus?

Flavius Josephus, the greatest Jewish historian, who lived not long after Jesus' own day, described his impact:

"About this time there was a wise man who was called Jesus. And his conduct was good and he was known to be virtuous. And many people from among the Jews and from the other nations became his disciples. Pilate condemned him to be crucified and to die.

"And those who had become his disciples did not abandon his discipleship. They reported that he had appeared to them three days after his crucifixion and that he was alive."

■ How does Jesus compare with other "leaders"?

Only a handful of men have founded world-changing movements, and most of them spent a long time teaching and recruiting before they did:

CONFUCIUS died 479 BC, aged 72
GAUTAMA BUDDHA died 483 BC, aged 80
MUHAMMAD died AD 632, aged 62
KARL MARX died AD 1883, aged 64

Jesus spent only three years teaching before dying, aged 33. He died as a criminal, with just a few hundred followers. Yet within 300 years belief in Jesus had gripped the Roman Empire. Today Christianity is by far the world's most widespread religion.

■ Did Jesus actually perform miracles?

The interesting thing is that *no-one living at that time attempted to deny it*. The Jewish Talmud attributed his miracles to Satan; the pagan philosopher Celsus said it was black magic; but *nobody* tried to say they hadn't happened. Perhaps because they were too well known to be doubted?

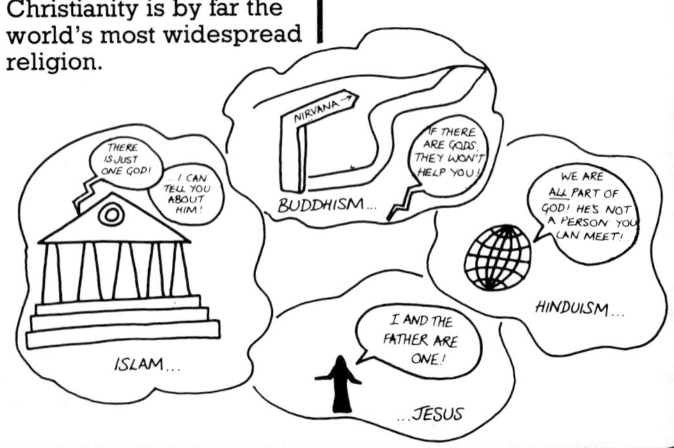

TAKE IT FURTHER

How to find out more.

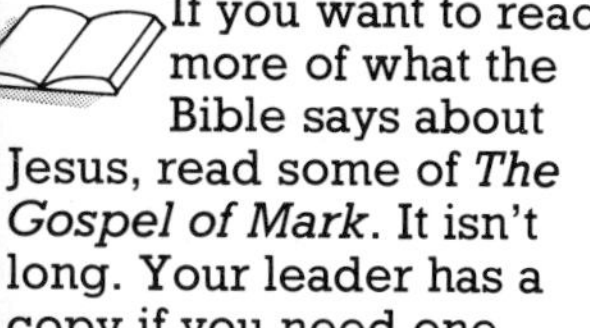

If you want to read more of what the Bible says about Jesus, read some of *The Gospel of Mark*. It isn't long. Your leader has a copy if you need one.

There's an extra **Factsheet** on the evidence for Jesus which your leader will be glad to give you. Just show on your **Reply card** that you'd like it.

Try out the "Jesus report" questions on a few of your friends. It's interesting to see what people really know about Jesus.

OVER TO YOU

This section is **FOR YOUR EYES ONLY** you don't have to show it to anyone else! But you can if you wish.

You've had a good look at Jesus. What do you think at the moment? Tick the boxes that best express your opinion.

I THINK THAT . . .

- ☐ Jesus was a good man, but not what he claimed to be.
- ☐ Jesus was either mad or evil, but not good, and not God.
- ☐ Jesus really was what he claimed to be — one with God.
- ☐ I'm still not certain because

____

AND SO . . .

- ☐ I'll keep my mind open, and carry on investigating.
- ☐ I've decided I want to be a Christian and follow Jesus properly.
- ☐ I'm not prepared to look any further. I want to give up **Just Looking** now.
- ☐ I'd like to ________________________________

JESUS' MISSION – WAS IT A FAILURE?

STARTER

Good news, bad news

Note here how many of the newspaper stories you found were:	Number of stories
Bad news caused by natural disasters (earth-quakes, volcanoes, etc.)	
Bad news caused by chance events	
Bad news caused by imperfect people	

BIBLE DATA

Did Jesus have any answer to the problem of imperfect people? Read this passage from John 3.1–9.

1There was a Jewish leader named
Nicodemus, who belonged to the party of the
Pharisees. 2One night he went to Jesus and
said to him, "Rabbi, we know that you are a
teacher sent by God. No one could perform
the miracles you are doing unless God were
with him."
3Jesus answered, "I am telling you the
truth: no one can see the Kingdom of God
unless he is born again."
4"How can a grown man be born again?"
Nicodemus asked. "He certainly cannot enter
his mother's womb and be born a second
time!"
5"I am telling you the truth," replied Jesus.
"No one can enter the Kingdom of God
unless he is born of water and the Spirit. 6A
person is born physically of human parents,
but he is born spiritually of the Spirit. 7Do not
be surprised because I tell you that you must
all be born again. 8The wind blows wherever
it wishes; you hear the sound it makes, but
you do not know where it comes from or
where it is going. It is like that with everyone
who is born of the Spirit."
9"How can this be?" asked Nicodemus.
(John 3.1–9)

BACKGROUND

- The "Pharisees" were a group of enthusiastic religious people who thought that the way to please God was to keep all his rules as strictly as possible. That led them to add an extra 693 rules to those already in the Old Testament.

  Nicodemus was a Pharisee, so he had tried living that way, but obviously wasn't satisfied. No matter how he tried, he knew he wasn't good enough to be sure of getting into God's kingdom.
- The fact that he went "at night" might show how eager he was to meet Jesus, or how scared he was of being seen talking to Jesus publicly.

REACTIONS

1. **Are there any things you don't understand about this passage, and would like explained?**
2. **Nicodemus might have been expecting Jesus to give him some new rules to keep. Instead, what did Jesus say he needed?**
3. **Looking at the passage, which of these comments do you think Jesus would disagree with?**
4. **Think about what babies are like. Why do you think Jesus used the phrase "born again" to describe the change people need?**
5. **Do you think Nicodemus understood Jesus? How do you think Nicodemus felt?**
6. **Is there anything else in this passage which you want to discuss before moving on?**

You can't change human nature!

Well, nobody's perfect!

You can only do your best!

BACK-UP DATA

• How do people change when they are "born again"? See how Paul describes a Christian's new life in Ephesians 4.17–32.

• How does God think about us when we're "born again"? See one example in 2 Corinthians 5.16–19.

FACT-FILE

■ What were the first Christians like?

The first Christians amazed everybody by the spectacular changes in their lives. That's one reason why Christianity spread so fast. The philosopher Aristides, writing in AD 125, said:

"They walk in all humility and kindness, and falsehood is not found among them, and they love one another. They despise not the widow, and grieve not the orphan. He that hath, distributeth liberally to him that hath not. If they see a stranger, they bring him under their roof, and rejoice over him, as it were their own brother . . ."

■ Was the idea that "Jesus is God" just a legend which grew and became distorted with time?

In 1868 a Roman inscription, dating from the century after the time of Christ, was dug up in Cirencester, Gloucestershire.

It was a word square:

ROTAS
OPERA
TENET
AREPO
SATOR

In this form it doesn't mean much. But scholars found they could rearrange it to spell the Latin word "paternoster" which means "our father" in two directions, in the shape of a cross. They realized it was a secret sign of the first Christians, showing that they believed, *right from the start*, that Jesus' death wasn't a failure — but the victory of God the Father on the cross. It was no garbled legend, but the basic belief of some of the earliest Christians.

■ Is it just Christians who believe people need a changed character?

Many great thinkers have agonized over the problem of how people can be given a new life. The scientific genius Albert Einstein, for example, wrote:

"The true problem lies in the hearts and thoughts of men . . . What terrifies us is not the explosive force of the atomic bomb, but the power of the wickedness of the human heart, its explosive power for evil."

TAKE IT FURTHER

If you started reading Mark's Gospel last time, keep going!

You'll also find Jesus talks about the problem of imperfect people in chapter 7, verses 20–23.

Your leader can give you a copy of a basic booklet which explains how to be "born again", or a **Factsheet** called "Why are there problems in the world?" Fill in the spaces on your **Reply card.**

"Watch" yourself for a couple of days. Note the way you react to people; spend your time and money; do things wrong. Then make a list of the changes you think God might have to bring about if you were "born again".

OVER TO YOU

What do you think about Jesus now? Tick the boxes that express your opinion.

This section is
FOR YOUR EYES ONLY
you don't have to show it to anyone else! But you can if you wish.

I THINK THAT . . .

- ☐ Jesus was wasting his time — human beings will someday become able to live good lives.
- ☐ Jesus was right about human nature, but his death hasn't changed anything.
- ☐ Jesus really did make it possible for human beings to have a new life.
- ☐ I'm still not certain because ______________________________

AND SO . . .

- ☐ I need to keep thinking for a while.
- ☐ I've decided I need to be born again.
- ☐ I know I should be born again, but I don't want to try it yet.
- ☐ I'd like to ______________________________

NEXT TIME

See you then.

CHRISTIANITY— CAN YOU BE SURE IT'S TRUE?

STARTER

I know for a fact . . .

Put the following statements in order of certainty. That is, put a "1" by the statement that you are *most certain is true*, a "2" by the next, and so on.

The moon is not made of green cheese		There are no holes in the group leader's socks	
Julius Caesar actually existed		I have four fingers and a thumb on my left hand	
There is life on other planets		Tottenham Hotspur F.C. are the world's greatest football team	

Just looking

LEADERS' NOTES

to be removed from group members' copies

your chance to believe it — or not

Just Looking is tested and tried. It works. Have confidence in the material and you will find it will repay the effort you put in.

The notes that follow are based on the experience of running **Just Looking** groups in many different environments. They are in three sections:

A **Before you start** — basic information for group leaders (Leaders' notes pages 1–4).
B **Detailed notes** — step-by-step through every session (Leaders' notes pages 4–13).
C **Resources** — reply card, reminder letter, and fact sheets (Leaders' notes page 14).

A. BEFORE YOU START

When to use Just Looking

A **Just Looking** group should consist of no more than five group members, plus a leader. Hard experience has convinced us of this. Keep it small. If some people can't get in, and have to be kept waiting, what a terrific advertisement for Christianity!

You will need a copy of this book for every group member. Remove these Leaders' notes (all the "tinted" centre section) from the members' copies. But don't throw them away — you'll be giving some of the pages (Fact-sheets 1–3) to group members at later stages.

Just Looking can be used in many situations:

- As a natural outcome to any form of teen-age evangelism — experience shows it's **much** more effective than challenging kids to an on-the-spot decision.
- As an extra activity for members of an open youth club who have shown an interest in learning more.
- As a do-it-yourself small-group activity Christian teenagers can run for groups of their friends at school.
- For teaching small groups on a Christian house party or holiday conference.

Anywhere, in fact, where there are young people curious to explore Christianity, but unwilling to attend church or join a youth fellowship in order to find out. **Just Looking** is for the non-joiners.

In recruiting, I've found the most effective selling point to be that **Just Looking** introduces you to Christianity with:

- No boredom — just plain, straight talking
- No embarrassment — no hymn-singing or personal questions
- No pressure — nobody's trying to manipulate you.

Throughout the sessions you will find many points at which young people are asked to make up their minds about what they have heard so far. Don't duck these out of embarrassment. They won't be embarrassed unless you are. The aim is to give as many chances of response as possible. The more "entry points" for a teenager too nervous to take the first one offered, the better.

Where and when to meet

Fix on a definite time which will **not** be varied except in an emergency. It should be convenient to them even if it slightly inconveniences you — after all, it's only for five weeks, and how often do you get evangelistic opportunities like this? Send each member a reminder letter three days before each meeting. A form is suggested on page 14 of the Leaders' notes.

Meet somewhere comfortable — **not** a church hall; and free from distractions — **not** a school class-room in the lunch hour.

Put on some music at the start, to cover awkward pauses in conversation.

If you're offering refreshments, don't be elaborate — it embarrasses them, and don't let it cut into group time. Have refreshments ready right at the start — at the end is an alternative, but it will prolong the meeting and people may be discouraged from returning if you keep them too long.

Conduct of the meeting
Stick to an hour. If they have questions they want to discuss afterwards, that's fine, but ensure anyone who wants to leave feels free to do so, and never let it go beyond an extra half-hour. If you finish while they still want more, they'll be keen to return. Each week use the **Reply cards** (see page 14) to make it possible for them to request a meeting with you — over a lunch-hour Coke, maybe — to discuss questions they don't want to bring up in the group.

Keep the meeting moving. The time allocation of each section should be like this:

Starter: A simple activity to break the ice, and get discussion going.

Bible study: Consists of a **Bible passage**, **Background** information, **Reaction** questions, and **Back-up data**. The aim is to explore the Bible passage in as much depth as possible to establish what it really says, rather than what we might like it to say! The **Reaction** questions are all based on the passage. Encourage the group to look for their answers in the passage.

Discussion: This is the time to open up more general discussion. In each session there are **Diagrams** to help you, and **Discussion** questions to ask the group. In three of the sessions, half the discussion time will be given over to a special guest.

Reaction and assessment: This includes the features on the second two pages of each session. **Take it further** suggests how group members can find out more. **Fact file** provides various facts and observations on the subject of the session. **Over to you** is the group members' chance to decide what **they** think.

Start on time. It's not fair to keep four kids waiting for one other. If they come within the first twenty minutes, they'll catch up.

At first there may be embarrassment, and people may be too shy to talk or may giggle a bit. Don't worry: it's simply an escape valve, not a sign that they're playing you up.

Combat shyness by asking direct questions — "What do you think, Gary?"; or asking for a group vote — "How many of you would agree with that?"

Avoid patronising, over-obvious questions — "And what does the third word in verse five say we should do?"; and questions that demand only a "yes" or "no" answer, because that's all you'll get!

If discussion moves away from the subject, steer it gently back. If the group shows signs of wanting to discuss a subject which doesn't really fit into that session, arrange a time when you can cover it properly, and get back to where you should be.

Other points to remember
In sessions three, four, and five, as I've already mentioned, you invite along a guest. Between weeks four and five, you will be taking your group along to church with you. There are notes about these events in the detailed guide to each session (page 4 onwards), but you should start thinking about it as soon as possible.

When people become Christians . . .
How will you know? We want to make it as easy and natural as possible for group members to accept Christ, and then tell you about it. The likeliest possibilities are these:

- The group member hands back a **Reply card** asking you for a meeting, and in that meeting finds Christ.
- The group member hands back a **Reply card** stating that he or she has now become a Christian. Meet with them quickly to discuss the next stage.
- At the end of the course, the group member indicates on the **Reaction sheet** that he or she has become a Christian, or wants to.

Reply cards are postcards given out at each session (see page 14 of Leaders' notes, for how to create them). The group members can fill them out and leave them with you, or mail them back during the following week.

Of course, they can also come and speak to you directly; but postcards are a way of overcoming feelings of embarrassment.

What do you do when somebody becomes a Christian? That depends on the follow-up arrangements in use in your church or mission. Make sure you know exactly what follow-up you can offer. As the group leader you should be the best person to look after a group member who has just accepted Christ. So unless there are good reasons why you shouldn't be involved, be prepared for this responsibility.

After Just Looking has finished
Some of your group are likely to become Christians. After all, they came along in the first place because they were interested! But don't feel discouraged if none of them do, or if some drop out. You are there to give them **a chance to investigate**, for themselves. Their response is **their own affair**. And let them see that you care about them **even if** in the end they reject what you believe.

You may want to stay in touch in some way afterwards. Work that out to suit your circumstances, but remember that they may **not** want to stay in touch. They committed themselves for five weeks, but their promise of involvement does not extend beyond that. Don't hound them!

While you are running the group, there may be occasional activities you'd like to take them to — a Christian concert, say. Always offer this as an option "if anybody's interested". Never make it seem that belonging to the group obliges them to attend this extra function. Otherwise your drop-out rate will be much higher!

Generally

Show interest in their lives and how they spend their time. Don't be too inquisitive, but remember things they tell you. Get to know them as people, not just group members. The discussions will flow more freely if you spend a few minutes before the official start-time of a meeting chatting about how they've spent the week, and what's happening to them. Share what's been happening to you, too. You may think your world is light-years away from theirs, but they do want to understand how **you** tick, what **your** interests are, how **you** approach life.

Involve your marriage partner, if you've got one. Group members of the opposite sex to yourself may find it easier to confide in your spouse. It will also help to prevent any embarrassing infatuations developing.

Don't visit their parents unless asked to. Young people do not appreciate this. It will seem like a conspiracy of adults. But show interest in their families and be available to the parents should they request a meeting.

Suppose they stop coming?

Hopefully, this won't be a major problem because:

- Everyone who applies for the course agrees to stick with it for five sessions and one church outing.
- The small size of the group means that absentees will be noticed very quickly, and that may help to keep them coming.
- If you send them a reminder each week, they have no excuse for just forgetting.
- If you are picking them up from home to bring them to the meeting, they will be much more likely to come.

But kids being kids, there will still be some drop-outs. What's the answer?

1. Get hold of anyone who didn't turn up and **talk to them** (don't just write), **casually** (don't make a big deal of it) and **privately** (don't embarrass them in front of parents and friends). It's not a good idea to visit them at home. Better to ring them up and ask if you can meet for a coffee somewhere in town. Or get a Christian kid at their school to fix up some such arrangement.
2. If they then turn up, you have a chance to renew contact and chat about how they're finding things, as well as encouraging them to come next time and filling them in on what the group did in their absence. If they don't turn up, don't push things. Just keep sending reminders of the next two meetings. If they don't respond, and it seems they have lost interest, drop them a note saying you're sorry they haven't found it possible to continue with the course, but you enjoyed meeting them and they'll always be welcome to drop in at your home.
3. In some situations, you could make a member of the group an "attendance officer", responsible for reminding people about meetings and rounding them up for you. Best if this member is **not** a committed Christian! But don't let anyone else send out the reminders. Do that yourself.
4. **Don't** resort to contacting the parents of a youngster who is irregular in attendance. Parents may well ensure they attend for the rest of the course, then they will come with a grudge, and learn nothing. Members' decisions to sign up were their own affair; parents were not involved. So don't drag them in later on to wield the big stick for you.
5. The key to the whole thing is staying open and welcoming to kids who decide that this is not for them. It is easy for us to feel hurt and rejected when they vote with their feet to stay away; and the natural thing is just to let them disappear from our lives.

But if we are careful to build bridges of friendship, we may be able to keep up the relationship even if they reject our beliefs. And that's something God can use for the future.

What if you lose your whole group?

This is just possible, if they are all close friends and used to taking decisions together. In this situation:

- Work out who is the dominant member of the group — the opinion-former whom everybody else follows. Get him/her to talk honestly about why they haven't found the group helpful. Work out how you can get over the problem. Then enlist his/her help to get them all back.
- If this doesn't work, accept defeat, and don't be too discouraged. Teenagers are very easily influenced by peer pressure. It isn't that five individuals have each decided, on

their own, that they don't like what you're doing; it's just that the group has made its choice. Don't let the discouragement prevent you from trying again.

The most important way of keeping your group together is to pray for each member of it, individually and at length. How do you think Jesus kept such a varied bunch as his twelve together? What do you think those long nights of prayer on the mountainside were all about?

B. DETAILED NOTES ON EACH SESSION

Session 1: Jesus — who was he?

Aim: To present the idea that we can actually know some reliable facts about Jesus; and that these facts logically leave us with a choice: either Jesus was a madman, or a confidence trickster, or God. It doesn't make sense to say, "He was just a good man."

Preparation: Read the passages used in the session. Work out carefully **your** answers to the questions. Prepare a **Reply card** (page 14) and a copy of **Factsheet 1** — "The evidence about Jesus" (following page 14) for everyone. Prepare your diagrams — see **Discussion**. Get a few copies of Mark's Gospel in a modern version. Send out the reminders three days before the meeting.

Back-up reading: If you want to do some preparatory reading about the evidence for Jesus, good books are:
John Drane, **Jesus and the Four Gospels** (Lion, 1984) — an excellent assessment of Jesus.
Josh McDowell, **More than a Carpenter** (Kingsway, 1979) — packed with useful facts.

Starter: "The Jesus Report" involves answering some basic questions about Jesus — individually, or in two competing teams. You could give a Mars bar or something similar to the winner.

The questions:

1. Where was Jesus born?
   a. Bethlehem
   b. Nazareth
   c. Jerusalem

2. Did he have brothers and sisters?
   a. Older than himself
   b. Younger than himself
   c. He was an only child

3. How many years did he spend as a preacher?
   a. Fifteen
   b. Three
   c. Seven

4. Which of these stories did he **not** tell?
   a. Parable of the Good Samaritan
   b. Parable of the Two Fishermen
   c. Parable of the Ten Virgins

5. Which of these statements did he **not** make?
   a. Do not resist anyone who is evil.
   b. I have come not to bring peace but a sword.
   c. Do as thou wilt shall be the whole of the law.

6. How many followers did he have at the time of his death?
   a. Just over 100
   b. 500–700
   c. 2,000

7. For what crime was he condemned?
   a. Disturbing the peace
   b. Plotting revolution
   c. Blasphemy

8. Which of these miracles did Jesus **not** perform?
   a. Feeding the 5,000
   b. Feeding the 6,000
   c. Feeding the 4,000

9. How many people claim to follow Jesus today?
   a. 568 million
   b. 14 million
   c. 1,433 million

Answers: a b b b c a c b c

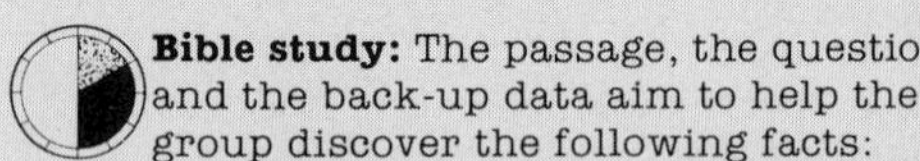

Bible study: The passage, the question and the back-up data aim to help the group discover the following facts:

- Jesus clearly claimed to be more than a man.
- He identified himself with God the Father, in his words and actions.
- He confidently assumed he knew more than those around him.
- He claimed authority to decide people's eternal future.

It is difficult, therefore, to dismiss him simply as a "good man".

Do not make these points yourself. Ask questions which will enable the group to explore the Bible passage for themselves.

Begin by reading the passage yourself, or

ıave it on tape beforehand, read by someone ılse. On no account ask them to read it aloud; ʼou will just embarrass them. **Back-up data** ʼerses, on the other hand, could be read by ;roup members. Type each one on to a slip ɪf paper, distribute them at the start of the ession to various people, and ask them to ead theirs out at the appropriate moment.)on't **ever** spring it on them! Don't expect hem to find verses for themselves in a Bible; nost will have no idea where to look.

The **Background** information can be eferred to if someone raises a question about he reliability of the Bible.

Discussion: You should have prepared a large (A4 or larger) version of the three diagrams below. Explain them one by one, before opening up the discussion.

Diagram 1.1

'his puts together some things we can say bout Jesus.

His teaching was brilliant — more original han anything for 700 years.

His subject was honesty; his greatest oncern was total integrity.

His standards were impeccable. None of his etractors could find any "dirt" to drag up bout him. His claim to perfection seems at əast possible.

His life-style was dedicated to helping thers; he gained nothing for himself.

His claim was disconcertingly simple: he ʋas equal with God.

sk the group:

Which of these facts doesn't seem to fit with the others?

Diagram 1.2

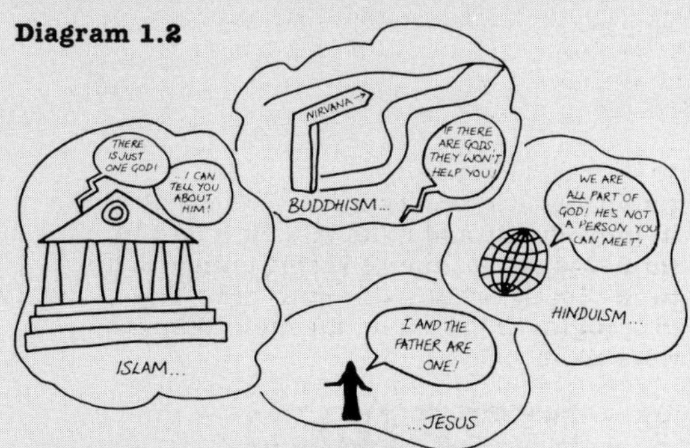

This compares Jesus with the founders of other great religions.

Muhammad claimed that there was only one God, and Muhammad was just his prophet who received messages from him.

Buddha claimed that if there was a God or gods, it was of no use to human beings. They had to struggle through life without help. Buddha was a teacher with helpful ideas.

Hindu teachers often claimed that all people were part of God, but God was just a force — not a person whom you could meet or talk to.

Jesus alone claimed equality with God. He lived in a culture where people were taught from their earliest years that there was only one God, with no rivals. So if he was lying, he hadn't picked a very plausible story!

Diagram 1.3

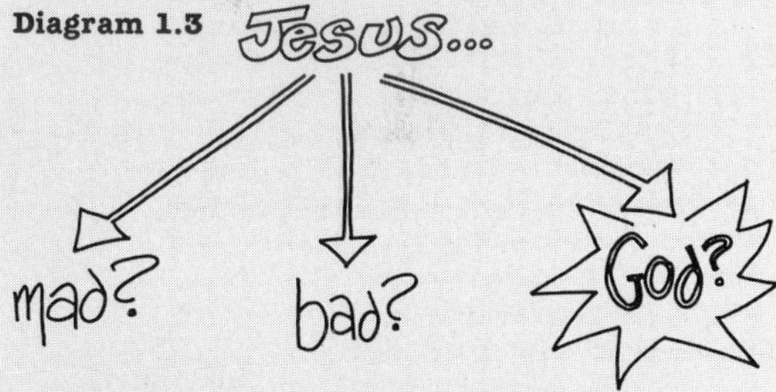

This points out the choice.

Was Jesus mad? His disciples were close to him for three years and never noticed. If they had suspected madness, which Jews feared as a curse from God, they'd have left him instantly. His teaching was brilliant, sane, and consistent. His behaviour was never erratic or excitable. He lived under great pressure, always in the spotlight, but showed no signs of instability.

Was Jesus bad? What did he stand to gain? A trickster would have recanted and signed a confession rather than have been crucified. Jesus gained neither money nor power by his efforts. And a con man would have come up with a less offensive, more plausible story.

Ask the group:

Can you think of any more reasons why Jesus couldn't have been mad or evil?

Would Jesus have been more effective if he'd just done some teaching and kept quiet about his identity?

Do you think it was easier for people in those days to swallow the idea that a person could be God — or was it more difficult?

When everybody has had a chance to share opinions and ideas, take two minutes — no longer — to summarize crisply what the choices are about Jesus, and that the evidence suggests he may have been what he claimed.

Reaction and assessment: Ask the group to look at the second spread of the session. **Take it further** suggests how they can find out more. Stress that this is optional.

Get them to read through **Fact file** on their own, and then fill in **Over to you**. Stress that this is "private" and "honest". They can fill in their own answers under the fourth option if none of the statements are right for them. They should also fill in the **Reply card** you have given them and return it to you. At that point the session is over.

Resist the temptation to open or close in prayer, sing choruses, etc., unless you want to embarrass them and lose them. This is not a religious service, and they are not committed believers. Do lots of praying, but before they come! In all the five sessions, there will be just one prayer — right at the end. The only exception will be if **all** the group become Christians before the end of the course. At that point you can ask them if they want to continue, or switch to a course for new believers instead. Even if they choose to continue, you can begin to incorporate elements of prayer and worship. **But this is the only situation** in which you should pray or sing with your group.

Session 2: Jesus' mission — was it a failure?

Aim: To convey the idea that our basic human problem is sin, that Jesus came to make new birth possible; and that the cross was where he achieved the possibility of a new life for us.

Preparation: Get hold of a pile of old national daily newspapers — the more the better; and some large pieces of paper or card, at least 2′×3′. Old wallpaper would do. Have scissors, Sellotape, and glue handy. Read through the Bible study material. Prepare one copy for each person of: **Factsheet 2** — "Why are there problems in the world?" and a **Reply card**. Obtain enough copies of a booklet describing what a Christian is. Your denomination's headquarters or a local Christian bookshop should have something suitable to use. If you haven't yet supplied all the materials requested on last week's **Reply cards**, have them ready to give out at the meeting. Send out meeting reminders three days before.

Back-up reading: The following books may help you with questions raised at the session:
Richard Bewes and Robert Hicks, **God, Man and Salvation** in "Explaining Bible Truth" series (Creative Publishing, 1981).
Paul Little, **Know what you believe** (Scripture Union, 1973).

Starter: Individually or in teams, people leaf through papers and cut out "bad news" stories (wars, famines, price rises, bank robberies, etc.) and stick them to their large piece of card, in an attempt to produce the most horrific newspaper front page they can manage. If they want it to look more like a real newspaper front page, they can draw a masthead at the top. The winner is the one who gets the most doomful stories on there in five minutes.

Then ask them to count up how many of their stories are bad news because of:

- Some natural disaster.
- Some chance event.
- Something done wrong by a human being.

They should enter the totals in the spaces on page 10.

You'll usually find, when you compare results, that there are far more "imperfect people" stories. Then discuss the two questions on the worksheet.

The point should emerge that a lot of our problems are created by our own fallen nature; and that the problems are virtually impossible to solve, unless we as individuals can be changed.

Bible study: It's a tricky passage, particularly the explanations of the water and the Spirit, so do make sure you give **Reaction** questions 1 and 6 a chance! You will also probably need to be ready to explain the term "Kingdom of God".

The discoveries that the questions should allow are:

- People can't change themselves by will-power.
- External changes are ineffective; an internal change needs to take place, and it's as radical as being born all over again.
- Jesus was talking about an invisible, non-

physical change which happens at the very centre of our personality.

● The agent of this change is the Holy Spirit. You may have to explain very simply who the Holy Spirit is, but don't get side-tracked into a detailed discussion of the Trinity at this point.

If opportunity allows — but don't force it — you may be able to share a bit of your own "new birth" story. But don't preach. Do it to draw out questions, not kill discussion! Share only a few details at first, then let them question you about the rest.

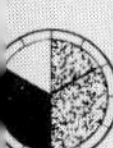

Discussion: Three diagrams launch the discussion:

Diagram 2.1

The problem. We are created in God's image, but cut off from God by sin. That means we're guilty, needing forgiveness; lost, needing to be found; dissatisfied, needing a purpose; helpless, needing power.

Diagram 2.2

Jesus claimed to be different. A real man, but also God. He had all the perfection of God and never did anything sinful. So there was no barrier between him and God. He was able to claim, as we saw in the last session, that he had a close relationship to the Father and knew his will better than anyone else living.

Diagram 2.3

When Jesus died, a great transfer took place. The sins which separated us from God were laid on him. He paid our penalty so that we could go free. Look at 1 Peter 2.24 or 2 Corinthians 8.9 here. Stress that this diagram isn't the end of the story. Jesus rose from death and went back to the Father. His separation from God is now over because everything has been settled — see Colossians 2.13–15.

Ask the group:

Isn't this unfair? Shouldn't we pay for our own misdeeds?

Many people still assume that we have to live a good life in order to **earn** God's approval. Can you see why people find that an attractive idea?

If Jesus did all this for us, does that mean we're all automatically forgiven? Or do **we** have to do something about it too?

Draw out opinions. If they're hesitant about expressing their own ideas, ask what they've heard other people say on this subject — they'll find that less risky! Make sure they've all understood what you've said. Ask questions which will reveal to you whether they've grasped it or not. Then, when you're sure they've got it, move on to the reaction and assessment.

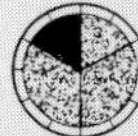

Reaction and assessment: Get them to read through **Fact file** and **Take it further** before filling in **Over to you** and the **Reply card**.

Session 3: Christianity — can you be sure it's true?

Aim: To explain what's supposed to happen when a person becomes a Christian; to discover that Christian faith, while based on good evidence about Jesus, is also a personal experience, and that this experience provides the clinching proof that faith is not just wishful thinking.

Preparation: Recruit guest 1. Ask a Christian friend to come to the meeting and talk **very briefly** — three minutes — about what has happened in their life to convince them that Christianity is true. It might be answered prayer, a change of character, a new power in living — anything. Your guest can be of any age, but must be the sort who can communicate well with young people, and be an attractive "advertisement" for Christianity. Warn them that after speaking they will be interrogated by the young people, with no holds barred, for up to ten minutes. Although their contribution is brief, they should be there for the whole meeting, and get to know the kids by name before the meeting begins. But they shouldn't attempt to contribute to the discussion before it is their time to come in. Unless, that is, the young people ask them directly what they think!

Note that you will need to supply another Christian guest — preferably a contrasting type of person — for session 4, and invite your pastor or a church leader to come along in session 5. Why not invite them **now** to make sure they'll be free? But first look at the notes for sessions 4 and 5 to ensure that you invite the right sort of person. I mention it now because it is good to consider all your three guests at the same time.

Read through the Bible study material. Work out how **you** would answer the **Starter**. Find out if the books mentioned in **Take it further**, or others like them, are in your local Christian bookshop, and how much they cost. If appropriate, you could even borrow some on sale or return, and display them to the group. Make sure you have enough **Reply cards**, and copies of the simple explanatory booklet on Christian faith. Send out meeting reminders.

Back-up reading: On how you can be sure about Christianity:
John Allan, **Sure Thing** (Kingsway, 1981).
Clark Pinnock, **Reason Enough** (Paternoster, 1980).
On evidence for the resurrection:
Michael Green, **The Day Death Died** (IVP, 1982).

Starter: The aim is to get the group thinking about what kinds of things we take to be proven.

First of all give them thirty seconds to each list as many **absolutely certain facts** as they can think of. The winner is the one who lists the most, but if any of those mentioned is not **certain**, a point is deducted.

Then get them to look at the six statements listed on page 14, and put them in order of certainty. Compare results. "Four fingers and a thumb" will probably come out top, because it is something we can verify directly with our eyes. "Julius Caesar" and "the moon" will come high because although we can't experience these facts directly, we have lots of reliable witnesses who have told us. "Life on other planets" is difficult because there is conflicting evidence. "The group leader's socks" would be verifiable if only people knew a little bit more than they do. "Spurs F.C." is just an unprovable expression of opinion. Analyse all this, using the questions below the **Starter**, and establish these points together:

- **Reliable witnesses** are important in helping us decide what to believe.
- **Good evidence** helps too (for example we have documents about Caesar).
- But the most certain thing of all is **direct experience**.

Then make a link — something like, "Tonight we decide whether when Christians say, 'My beliefs are true', is that just:

An expression of opinion? ('Tottenham Hotspur'.)

Something that could be right or wrong? ('Life on other planets'.)

Something founded on good evidence and reliable witnesses? ('Julius Caesar'.)

Or something you can test out in direct experience? ('Four fingers and a thumb'.)"

Bible study: This is more difficult than any of the other passages so far. The questions help group members discover that:

- Salvation depends on God's free gift, not our efforts.
- It does not automatically mean a life free from problems.
- A step of faith is necessary for us to receive God's gift.
- When we accept new life from God, certain changes take place which help to assure us that it's all true.

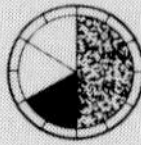

Discussion: Half of the time will be devoted to your diagrams, **half** to the special guest.

Diagram 3.1

To prove that a claim is true, you must prove that it is supported by **evidence** and **experience**. Suppose lawyers want to prove that the prisoner in the dock is guilty of murder. They'll assemble evidence: the blood-stained knife with fingerprints on; the fact that the prisoner has no alibi; the hate letter sent to the murder victim a month beforehand. But if they can produce **experience** too — a witness who was there and saw the crime being committed — they've really sewn up the case. In the same way, Christianity has a lot of **evidence** behind it. For example, the evidence for the resurrection has convinced sceptics that Jesus was God. But the most convincing thing is the **experience** which you can have.

Diagram 3.2

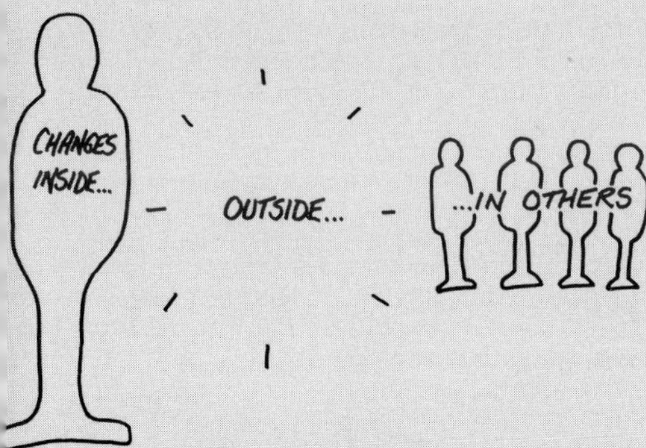

Inner experiences such as peace, joy, or satisfaction are part of it. But could they be simply wishful thinking? No, because there are also changes **outside** of yourself, in circumstances over which you have no control. Things like answered prayer, "coincidences" that happen too often to be merely chance. These aren't feelings, but facts. And, third, you see the same kind of experience **in other people**. When you get to know other Christians, of differing age, mentality, nationality, and background, you find the same Jesus doing the same things in them. It all helps to show that it's not just wishful thinking, but solid reality.

Ask the group:

Would it be even **more** certain if Jesus materialized in front of you and did a miracle?

Are there good reasons for him keeping out of sight? Would it be easier or harder to believe if all sorts of unexpected or strange things were constantly happening?

The second half of the discussion is devoted to your **special guest.** Introduce your guest briefly. Explain that he/she has been arrested on suspicion of believing something completely illogical, and has three minutes to convince the jury (the group) that's not true. Afterwards they will cross-examine him/her. The time limit is strict. At the three-minute mark, stop the guest dead! Then open up the cross-examination.

Reaction and assessment: Read **Fact file** and **Take it further** and fill in **Over to you** and a **Reply card** as usual.

Session 4: Being a Christian — what is it like?

Aim: To communicate the challenge of genuine Christian living; to introduce the Holy Spirit's work in the Christian.

Preparation: Recruit guest 2. All the qualifications for guest 1 still apply — i.e. you need someone who can communicate well with young non-Christians. Guest 2 has three minutes (strictly-timed) to describe:

- What the Holy Spirit has done in his/her life.
- How he/she tries to be "salt" and "light" in daily living.

After this, the group interrogate the guest, as they did at the last session. **This means that your ideal guest is someone who is conspicuously "salt" and "light" in the community — that is, someone who is actively trying to make a difference in the world — who perhaps is working with difficult people at great personal cost.** Don't choose someone who identifies the Holy Spirit's working with experiences which are bizarre and difficult for non-Christians to understand.

Read through the Bible study material. Familiarize yourself with the **Starter**. Make sure you have enough **Reply cards** and copies of a booklet of basic advice for new Christians (from your church headquarters or local Christian bookshop). Send out meeting reminders. This is also the week for the church trip — read the notes about it, that follow the notes on this session.

Back-up reading: On Christian life:
Jim Wallis, **The Call to Conversion** (Lion, 1982).
David Watson, **Discipleship** (Hodder & Stoughton, 1983).
On the work of the Holy Spirit:
J. I. Packer, **Keep in Step with the Spirit** (IVP, 1984).
On the record of Christians through history:
Heritage of Freedom (Lion, 1984).

Starter: This is an exercise to get the group thinking about how a Christian might react in certain situations. Below are outlines of some every-day situations. The group try to spot a Christian approach to the situation and write their answer in the appropriate space on page 18. Make two things clear: First, that this is not how Christians always behave — but how they might; and second, that you're not saying that only Christians would act in this way — just that these reactions are typical of what Christian experience should produce in someone's life.

The following list does not follow the order given on page 18 of the session, for good reason.

1. Three drivers, on a busy road, come upon an accident. No-one is hurt but the driver of the car which has hit a telephone pole is standing by the roadside wondering what to do next. G drives on, saying, "I'm too busy to stop. And anyway, it's raining." H stops and tries to help; so does I. The grateful driver offers them money. I accepts; H doesn't. Which of them showed the most "Christian" behaviour? (H)
2. The supermarket check-out girl is having a bad day, and adding everything up wrongly. She charges S too much, who points this out. She also charges T too much, but he doesn't like to complain, so he suffers in silence. But when she overcharges U, he explodes with anger and threatens to call the police. Which of them showed the most "Christian" behaviour? (S)
3. A mother asks her three sons, A, B, and C, to do the washing up. A points out that it isn't his turn. B admits that it is his turn, but he's going out and can't stop to keep his promises. C is going out too, but he waits long enough to do the washing up. Which of them showed the most "Christian" behaviour? (C)
4. The teacher leaves the room, but warns the class that they have to work quietly till she comes back. As soon as she's gone, S starts making a racket. T carries on working, and so does U, but when U thinks she has done enough to satisfy the teacher she stops and joins in with S. Which of them showed the most "Christian" behaviour? (T)
5. Three friends go to a party. P gets wildly drunk. Q eggs him on to drink more, and laughs at him. R keeps advising him to go home, and in the end escorts him there. Which of them showed the most "Christian" behaviour? (R).
6. J accuses I and K of pushing in front of him in the cinema queue. They answer that they were there first. J becomes abusive, and as a result the other two let J go in front. I says, "Never mind, J's probably having a bad day." But it spoils K's evening who grumbles about J's nerve. Which of them showed the most "Christian" behaviour? (I)

The six answers should spell out the secret of real Christian living: C H R I S T. **You can, if you wish, invent other scenarios closer to the experience of the group** — ensure, however, that you fix it so that your answers still spell out the word Christ.

Explain that living this way isn't something Christians do by themselves — Christ helps them to live on a new level.

Bible study: The aim of the passage and the questions is to present Christian living as a positive challenge — not sitting still and singing hymns, but changing the world.

- Christians are **salt** in the community — preserving it as they stand for morality, equality, and justice, as they spread love and make peace.
- They are also **light**, helping people see the glory of God through the good deeds they perform.

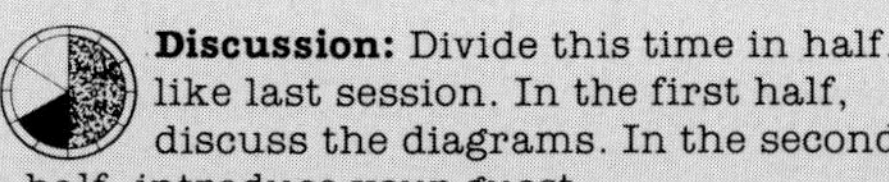

Discussion: Divide this time in half, like last session. In the first half, discuss the diagrams. In the second half, introduce your guest.

Diagram 4.1

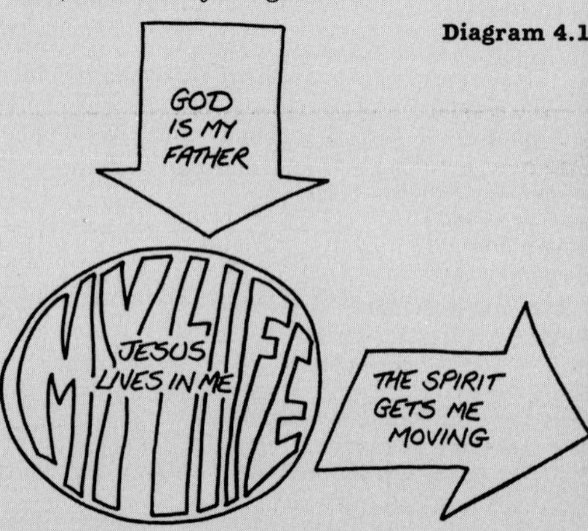

This shows how the Holy Spirit makes Christians into new people — building the life and character of Jesus into our lives. The Father cares for us; Jesus lives in us; and the Spirit gives us energy.

Diagram 4.2

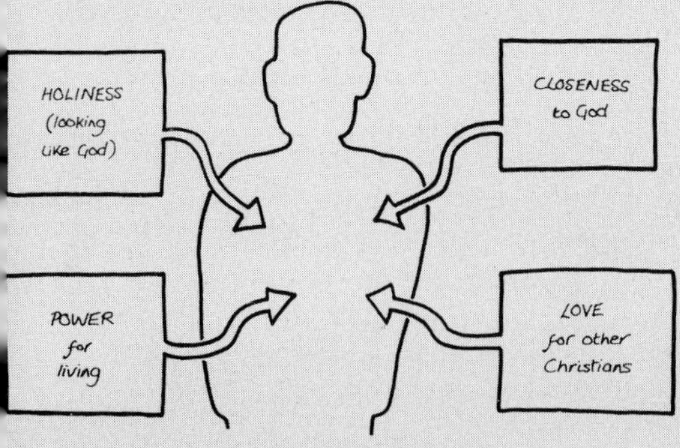

This shows some things the Holy Spirit brings: holiness (which means a character reflecting God's); power for living and for God's service; love for other Christians (Romans 5.5); closeness to God (Romans 8.16 and 26).

Then ask the group:

Why is it that sometimes non-Christians seem to be better people than Christians? Does this disprove what we've been saying about the Holy Spirit?

If Christians are controlled by the Holy Spirit, why are some of them leading such unimpressive lives?

On the first question, note that Christians aren't necessarily better than other people — it all depends on how much natural goodness they started with! But they **will** be better than **they would have been** without Christ! On the second question, note that just because the power is there, it doesn't mean it's switched on. It's possible to **resist** the Holy Spirit, even if you're a Christian.

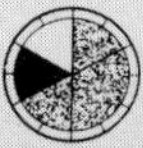
The second half of the discussion is devoted to your **special guest**. Introduce your guest. The brief is described in **preparation** above. Time him/her — three minutes is the deadline — then the group interrogates the guest, as they did in the last session.

Reaction and assessment: Read **Fact file** and **Take it further**. Then fill in **Over to you**, and a **Reply card**. Make arrangements for the church trip next Sunday.

THE CHURCH TRIP

– the Sunday after session 4

How to introduce it

'Well, this coming Sunday is when we do a bit of field work. It's alright sitting in a room and studying what a church **should** be like; but if you're going to understand it properly you need to see it in action. So this Sunday we visit a church together. And I want you to act like a Martian who's never seen anything like it before. Be as inquisitive as possible. Keep on the look-out for things that don't make sense, things you don't understand, things they could do better. Then afterwards we'll all have a good meal and discuss what you thought . . .''

What to do:

1. Plan carefully which church service you go to. It should be one which is lively, comparatively easy to understand, and likely to be of interest to unbelievers. Warn some of your friends that you will be bringing your group along. Make sure they are ready to introduce themselves, chat to the kids, and make them feel at home.

2. Show the group round the church premises, before or after the service, and explain to them what you do in the various rooms. There's often a mystique about churches which frightens young people. They look at them with the same kind of awed incomprehension that you might have for a Sikh temple or a Freemason's hall.

3. Arrange to pick your group up and take them to church if possible. Don't ever arrange to meet them **at** the church. It is important that you arrive at the church **as a group** and walk in together. Sit with them too. Don't be annoyed if they giggle a bit or swap stage-whisper comments; it's just embarrassment.

4. Give the group a running commentary throughout the service, on the bits they might find difficult to understand.
Don't allow them to get bored through incomprehension.

If you use service books with a confusing

number of pages, help them find the place, but do it unobtrusively, so that they don't feel everybody must be watching them.

If there are points in the service where people suddenly rise to their feet, or sit down, or kneel down, warn them it's coming well before it happens.

If your church has the practice of inviting people to leave their seats at one point in order to greet each other and shake hands, stick with them and introduce them to people; don't leave them to cope on their own.

If there are things which people sing (choruses, or sung responses) which aren't written down, give them a written copy before the service begins.

5. Don't confuse the group with denominational issues unless they ask. The point is to show them, "This is what a Christian church is like" — not to show them, "This is what makes us Pentecostals/Baptists/Anglicans better than inferior varieties . . ."

6. Afterwards, take the group off somewhere for a good meal — supper or lunch, depending on the time of service you've attended! — so that even if the service was a disaster they remember something nice about the trip! Remember that Sunday is often a family day for outings and the like, so they may not have too long to spare. Serve the meal quickly and let them go when they need to. But ensure that you analyse the service together, and get their instant reactions to it. Answer any immediate questions they have.

As you discuss, jot down:

- The questions they had about things they didn't understand.
- Their major criticisms of features they didn't like.
- Suggestions for improvements they might have.

You will be using this as the basis of discussion with a church leader in session 5.

And next . . . ?
One hopes that many of your friends, in chatting to the kids, have warmly invited them to come again next week. You may feel like doing the same, but **don't**! You took them to church, not as a way of enticing them into regular attendance, but as a one-off learning experience. So **leave it up to them**. If they want to come back, they'll tell you, without any need for you to nudge them into it!

Session 5: The Church — Christianity's worst advert?

Aim: To get group members to see beyond their prejudices and hang-ups about the church, and understand God's purpose in drawing Christians together. To show the creative potential of a church which aims to follow God's plan. To help members make a decision about Christian faith.

Preparation: For the **discussion** you will need to invite along either your pastor or a church leader. Have a look at the notes under **discussion** to help you decide whom to invite.

Read through the session. Send out reminders. Ensure you have enough **Reply cards** and copies of **Factsheet 3**, "How to go to church . . . and like it". Also get a polystyrene throw-away cup — not plastic — for each member of the group.

Starter: The great polystyrene cup massacre! Ask each person to do to a polystyrene cup what they'd like to do to the Church. Give an example, to get them started — punch holes in it to make it more open to the outside world? Give them five minutes, then go round the group getting them to explain what they've done!

Bible study: The aim of the Bible passage is to show the true purpose of the Church and the Christian. The questions help them:

- Understand **why** the Church is there. It isn't just a monument. It has real goals, aims, and purposes.
- Shatter some of the stereotypes about money, class, dress, and formality.
- See that just "going to church" is not enough. The Church is a family which shares its whole life together, or it is nothing.

Discussion: In the first half, use Diagram 5.1.

Diagram 5.1

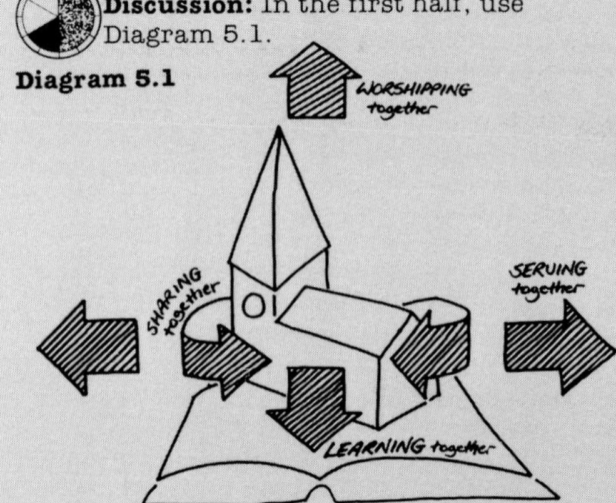

Jse this to discuss the four functions of the Church:

- Learning together.
- Serving together in the world, both in witness and in practical caring.
- Sharing together in encouragement, love, and practical ways.
- Worshipping together, helping one another to appreciate God.
- You may want to relate this specifically to your own church.

Ask the group:

Are there ways in which the Church could do its job better?

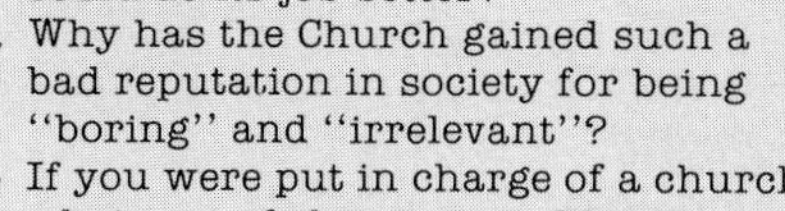
Why has the Church gained such a bad reputation in society for being "boring" and "irrelevant"?

If you were put in charge of a church, what sort of changes would you try to bring about?

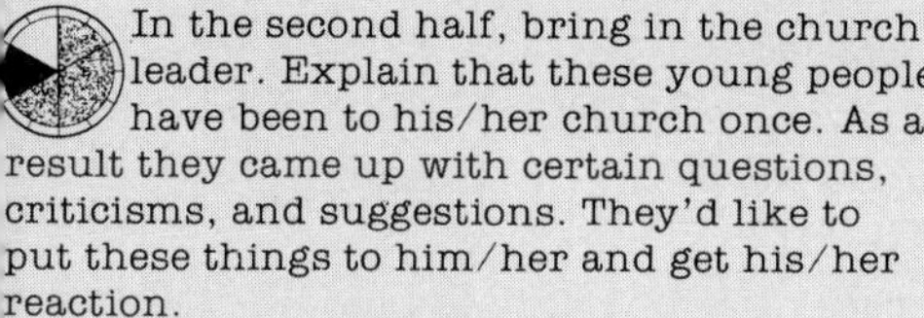
In the second half, bring in the church leader. Explain that these young people have been to his/her church once. As a result they came up with certain questions, criticisms, and suggestions. They'd like to put these things to him/her and get his/her reaction.

Make sure the church leader is not someone who feels threatened by the questions. They're not defending the church against hostile critics, but simply explaining to interested outsiders why things happen the way they do. The more open the leader is to their comments, the more likely they are to come back to the church! **This means that the church leader you choose needs to be someone who is fairly confident in talking to young people, flexible enough not to feel nettled by youthful criticism, and thoughtful enough to be able to make a reasonable case for the way things are done.** You may decide the pastor or vicar is less appropriate than a young leader. But don't upset anyone by your choice!

Reaction and assessment: Read **Fact file** and **Take it further**, and then leave a full ten minutes at the end for people to fill in **Over to you**. Remind them that this is the end. There's a lot more that could be said about Christianity, but they've had a reasonably good look, and now they need to decide where they stand. Get them to read very carefully **Over to you**. In some groups it may be good to read it aloud to them.

Say that you'd like to end your time together by giving them a chance to respond, if they want to, and accept Jesus Christ for themselves. You are going to pray a prayer, and they can join in and pray silently with you if they'd like to say "Yes!" to God's offer of new life.

Then pray something like this:

"Lord Jesus, I've heard a lot about you and I've gradually become convinced that I need to give you a chance with my life. I've looked at the claims of Christianity, and the cost involved in handing myself over to you, and I think I'm ready to invite you to give me a new life, born again into the family of God. I ask you to forgive me for the wrong that is in me and to make me the kind of person you always want me to be. Let me know that you are really there, and help me to live faithfully for you. Thank you for dying on the cross for me. Thank you for hearing my prayer and answering it."

Explain that if they prayed the prayer, they may feel no different — or they may feel totally transformed! It makes no difference, because it doesn't depend on feelings; a new life has started. But they need to get the best out of living that new life; to associate with God's people and start learning to live in the power of the Holy Spirit. So ask them, if they prayed the prayer, to see you or tick the **Reply card**. It is important that they don't try to struggle through on their own as "secret Christians".

On page 27 there is a **Reaction sheet** for each member to fill in. Get them to do it now if it seems appropriate.

The course is over. Stay in touch with your kids if you can. Even if they haven't accepted Christ, they now have more insight into the Gospel then most people; and God may use that some day.

What next?

Refer back to pages 2–3, concerning follow up. It might be good to bring things to an end with an unmistakable gesture which signals clearly that you still value those who have decided not to accept Christ — for example, throwing a party for the group, or giving them a present.

Meanwhile, **thank you for all your hard work**. We hope you found it rewarding and stimulating.

And we hope you'll do it again.

Write to me c/o the Bible Society address on page 2 and tell me how you got on. **You** can fill in the **Reaction sheet** on page 27 as well! We can constantly improve **Just Looking** if you share with us what was helpful/unhelpful in your particular situations.

C. RESOURCES

Reply card
At every session you will need to prepare **Reply cards** (see also page 2). These are the same every week, so you could prepare twenty-five at the start, to cover the whole course.

A sample **Reply card** appears below. It should ideally be on the back of a plain postcard. Add your own personal touches — for example your name, where it says "(leader's name)" on line one.

Reminder letter
You will need to send round a letter to each group member each week (see page 1). A suggested form appears below. Again, make it as personal as you can.

Factsheets
On the following three pages are copies of **Factsheets** 1, 2, and 3. Keep these safely until they are needed at sessions 1, 2, and 5. Group members ask for these when they fill in their **Reply card**. It is an important part of **Just Looking** that they should have to positively "ask" for more information. So don't give them out unless they're asked for.

Please give this card to (leader's name) at the end of the session, or send it to me in the course of next week.

Tick anything you want to, or leave it all blank if you have nothing to say.

I found this week's session:

- ☐ Absolutely brilliant
- ☐ quite interesting
- ☐ not very good, because:

☐ I would like the following things, which are mentioned in the 'TAKE IT FURTHER' section:

☐ I would like the following question answered next time:

☐ I would like to ask you some questions sometime. Let's meet for a coke and a chat.

My name: ______________

◄ Reply card

Dear

The next 'Just Looking' meeting is at ______________ on ______ at ______ p.m.

I'm looking forward to seeing you there as usual.

By the way, remember to keep ______ clear for the special 'CHURCH TRIP' we're going to have.
See you soon.

your chance to believe it — or not

FACT SHEET 1

The evidence for Jesus

What can you know — for *sure* — about Jesus Christ? If you believe everything you hear, you might think the answer is, "Not very much". Most people assume that there are so many myths and legends surrounding Jesus Christ, it's *impossible* to know the truth.

A few years ago most scholars would have agreed with them. But we've found out a lot of things this century which have shown that you can actually know a *great deal* about Jesus Christ. For instance:

He really lived

There's no possibility that he was just a myth. Jesus is mentioned by many non-Christian writers of the time:

Suetonius

Josephus

Tacitus

Pliny

Lucian

Thallus

Also, we now know that the Gospels were written too soon after Jesus died to have been fakes. People still remembered him very clearly, and wouldn't have swallowed a lot of exaggerated claims. One scholar, Professor J. Jeremias, has shown that the Gospels bear the traces of Jesus' own speaking style — it's as if we're listening to the voice of Jesus himself.

He was a brilliant thinker

You can't find any teacher equal to Jesus in any of the great minds of his day. It had been hundreds of years since the Jews had produced anyone with such a lively mind. And the statements of Jesus have been more quoted than any other words in history. Look in any dictionary of quotations, and check how much space is given to the words of Jesus Christ. He was unique. He was a genius.

He may well have been a miracle-worker

"Oh, come on", you might complain. "Water into wine?" Feeding five thousand people? You can't believe things like that. Obviously they were just legends which were made up afterwards." Well, it's interesting that Jesus' opponents didn't deny he had done some miraculous things. They claimed he'd done it all by the power of Satan — but they did admit he'd done it! A hundred years afterwards, one Christian writer told the Emperor Antoninus Pius that if he didn't believe the miracle stories, he only had to look in the official records of Pontius Pilate — it was all written down in there. Now we no longer have those records, so we can't look; but it would have been stupid for the Christian writer to make that claim if it *wasn't* all officially noted down!

He claimed to be perfect, and maybe he was

Even more incredible? Well, hang on. This was a claim which Jesus' followers made right from the very start. You find it all over the New Testament. All his enemies had to do was drag up one piece of dirt about him and his credibility would have been exploded. They never did. And remember that Jesus' followers were a very shrewd bunch of fishermen and peasants — people who knew how to see through fancy claims — and they spent three years travelling round with him, living closely with him, sleeping rough, sharing food and money. If Jesus had once done something morally bad, they'd have spotted it — and then left him.

He changed people's lives

The Bible claims that six weeks after Jesus' death, 3,000 people became his followers in one day in Jerusalem. Certainly we know that the Church spread rapidly — just as Jesus had predicted — all over the ancient world. Christianity began as a small sect with a handful of followers, and the Romans tried to stamp it out by killing believers and feeding them to the lions; but by 329 AD so many lives had been changed by Christianity that the Emperor gave in and made it the official religion of the Roman Empire!

Why was there such a tremendous impact on so many people? Because Christians believed Jesus had risen from the grave, was alive again, and could give people a new life. Nobody else could explain what had happened to the body of Jesus; it was a genuine mystery. And when thieves, prostitutes, philosophers, housewives, Roman governors, and Jewish priests all started to claim that this dead man had changed them into better people — the whole world had to sit up and take notice!

According to the *World Christian Encyclopaedia*, 59,200 people *every day* are having the life-changing experience of meeting Jesus. Could he change *your* life?

your chance to believe it — or not

FACTSHEET 2

Why are there problems in the world?

arthquakes. Famines. Thalidomide abies. Six million Jews obliterated in he Second World War. Auschwitz. elsen. Kampuchea. Uganda. Death, ain, and torture . . .

Why doesn't God stop it? Doesn't he care?

ome people have said, "No, he doesn't. here can't be a God. Life must be eaningless."

Brief and powerless is man's life; on im and all his race the slow, sure doom alls pitiless and dark. Blind to good and vil, reckless of destruction, omnipotent atter rolls on its relentless way . . ." ertrand Russell

ut is that really all there is to life? Or oesn't this solution leave us with *more* explain?

Suppose for a minute that the problem f pain drives you to reject God's xistence and to imagine that either ome monster rules our destinies or that he stars are in charge of our fortunes, ow does that help? You may have got id of the problem of evil and pain . . . ut you have replaced them with a much igger problem: how you get kindness nd humanity, love and unselfishness, gentleness and goodness in a world that is governed by a horrid monster or uncaring stars. No, that way does not help." Michael Green

If there is a good God, why is there so much suffering in the world?

The Bible gives us a few clues, although there are lots of things we don't understand. I don't know why a brilliant young Christian poet and rock singer I knew was allowed to die in a head-on car collision. I don't know why friends of mine have died agonizingly from cancer. But God has supplied a few ideas . . .

A lot of the problems in the world are caused by human beings

Don't blame God for Ulster. Or Vietnam. Or the St. Valentine's Day Massacre. *We* did those things, not him. Even the famines in the Third World are often a result of government corruption or the greed of the rich nations. Deformities in babies are often due to the greed of drug companies who don't test products properly.

So why doesn't God stop us? Because he has given us *freedom* — not made us mindless robots who would just blindly do whatever he commanded. It's his greatest gift, but it does have its dangers. It means we're free to do wrong things as well as right; and the problem of the world is that we all do wrong.

Human evil has ruined God's creation too

The Bible claims that when humans turned their backs on God, the whole of creation suffered. That's what Genesis 3.17–19 is talking about. This world doesn't work the way it should any more; it's "out of sync", and so you get natural disasters, pain, and suffering. The apostle Paul says that creation "groans with pain", looking forward to the day when Jesus returns to set everything right.

It hurts God just as much

God doesn't just stand there and watch while we suffer. It twists him up, too, that people he loves and created with care should be hurting so much. And when Jesus died on the cross, God himself was sharing in human suffering. He passed through it himself so that death could be defeated, human beings given new hope, and a new world eventually created.

This world is not always a pleasant place. But Jesus suffered so that he could give us hope that goes beyond the grave, and power for living — whatever problems we face.

FACT SHEET 3

How to go to church . . . and like it

'here can be a lot wrong with a church. 'he paint may be peeling off the walls nd the rain dripping through the roof. 'hey may all dress up in fancy clothes nd hold services in a language which ounds remotely like English, but you ouldn't swear to it. There may be old adies sucking peppermints on the back ow, and adult versions of the Milky Bar id dressed weirdly in flares, whom you night think you'd never be able to get n with in five hundred years.

Or it may not be like that at all. There is growing number of churches where umbers are high, the services are vely, lots of young people are involved, nd Sunday morning is the highlight of ne week.

But whatever your local church is like, ou need to realize some things about it:

t's not a place to attend, but family to belong to

he point of going to church is not to sit rough an hour of bottom-numbing oredom every Sunday so that God will nally let you into heaven! The point is at once you're a Christian you belong the family of God. And like in a human amily your brothers and sisters can help ou. So . . .

How not to survive:

- Just put in time at one of the services.
- "Clock off" for the week when it's over saying, "I've done my duty".

How to survive:

- Get as involved as possible with your new family.
- Get to know them, and spend time with them.

It's not an entertainment agency, but a job centre

If you judge church services purely as entertainment, they certainly don't match up to what you can get elsewhere — on TV or at a night club. But then the church isn't a show put on for the benefit of the congregation, while they sit back and watch and applaud at the end. The members of a church have been brought together by God to work together for his kingdom and help one another to grow as Christians. Look for somewhere which will give you a worthwhile, creative job to get stuck into.

How not to survive:

- Judge the services in terms of their star-rating for laughter and entertainment.
- Don't ever do anything more energetic than criticizing.

How to survive:

- Find a way, right from the start, of helping in the church's work.
- Get involved in helping to build God's kingdom.

It's not a pointless ritual, it's a growing body

The New Testament describes the Church as "the body of Christ". Like any other body, it has lots of different parts, but they all need to grow. A healthy church will be:

Learning together

A Church is built on what God has said. There's nothing wrong with social activities and save-the-steeple funds, but it's far more important to get to grips with God's dynamic message. Don't miss out on any opportunity to learn.

Worshipping together

Coming together to worship God is absolutely central to church-life. Worshipping God is like telling your girlfriend or boyfriend how much you love them — it strengthens the bond between you.

Sharing together

Church members can share together in practical ways, and also give encouragement and support to one another.

Serving together

Every Christian should help meet other's needs by sharing what they have, fighting injustice, and by telling the world about the reality of Jesus. But we can do it much more effectively together than on our own.

How not to survive:

- Go through the motions of church-going, without ever stopping to think what you're going there for.

How to survive:

- Make sure that your church is involving you in all the ways mentioned — learning, worshipping, sharing, and serving alongside other Christians.

BIBLE DATA

Vhat can Christians be sure about? Check out Romans 5.1 – 11.

1Now that we have been put right with God
:hrough faith, we have peace with God
:hrough our Lord Jesus Christ. 2He has
orought us by faith into this experience of
God's grace, in which we now live. And so
we boast of the hope we have of sharing
God's glory! 3We also boast of our troubles,
because we know that trouble produces
endurance, 4endurance brings God's
approval, and his approval creates hope.
5This hope does not disappoint us, for God
has poured out his love into our hearts by
means of the Holy Spirit, who is God's gift to
us.
6For when we were still helpless, Christ
died for the wicked at the time that God
chose. 7It is a difficult thing for someone to
die for a righteous person. It may even be
that someone might dare to die for a good
person. 8But God has shown us how much
he loves us — it was while we were still
sinners that Christ died for us! 9By his
sacrificial death we are now put right with
God; how much more, then, will we be saved
by him from God's anger! 10We were God's
enemies, but he made us his friends through
the death of his Son. Now that we are God's
friends, how much more will we be saved by
Christ's life! 11But that is not all; we rejoice
because of what God has done through our
Lord Jesus Christ, who has now made us
God's friends.
(Romans 5.1–11)

BACKGROUND

"Our troubles," verse 3. Many hristians faced opposition. Paul imself, the writer of this assage, was imprisoned, ship-recked, and tortured because of s Christian work. These are the roubles" he and other Christians ced.

Vhat some of the other important ords mean:

Faith — complete trust and onfidence in somebody.

Grace — kindness shown to omeone who doesn't deserve it.

Righteous person — omeone who has not done nything wrong.

Sinners — people who fail to ve a good life.

ASK YOURSELVES...

? **Which facts could you be more sure about if you have better information?**

? **Which facts is it impossible to know about — and why?**

REACTIONS

Are there any things you don't understand about this passage, and would like explained?

Which of these statements is wrong according to the passage? Explain why.

- You become a Christian by a step of faith
- Jesus died on the cross for righteous people
- Jesus' death gives us the chance of peace with God.

Something wrong here. What does this passage have to say about it?

What do we need to have, in order to be "put right with God"? What do you think this means we have to do?

According to these verses, being a Christian changes our past, present, and future. How?

Is there anything else in this passage which you want to discuss before moving on?

BACK-UP DATA

The Bible claims that we can be *sure* Christianity's claims are true because certain things start to happen to us after we become Christians. Listed below are three passages which talk about some of the experiences we can expect:

- 1 John 5.11–18
- Colossians 1.9–14
- 1 John 3.9–10

FACT-FILE

■ Are people really being "changed" by God these days?

One of the most publicized conversion stories of the last few years was that of Chuck Colson, the wily, tough lawyer who was one of the closest advisers of President Nixon in the USA. Colson was one of the leading politicians who were disgraced and sent to prison because of the Watergate scandal. Then his life changed direction. Now he's devoted his life to helping men in prison. He says in his book *Born Again* that he's found:

"... strength and serenity, a wonderful new assurance about life, a fresh perception of myself and the world around me. In the process, I felt old fears, tensions and animosities draining away. I was coming alive to things I'd never seen before ..."

■ Is Christianity dying out?

Around the world today, Christianity is changing more people than ever before. According to the best statistics available, the Church has grown from 558 million in 1900 to 1,433 million now. In Africa 16,400 people become Christians every day. There are 460 new churches in the world every week. During this century Christianity has become the first truly universal religion in history with Christian communities in all nations.

■ But does this change last?

Of the twelve first apostles, only one (John) died a natural death. The rest were tortured and flogged, and six were crucified. One was stoned, and the others died by the sword, spears, and arrows. None denied their faith. Clearly they were pretty sure about something.

TAKE IT FURTHER

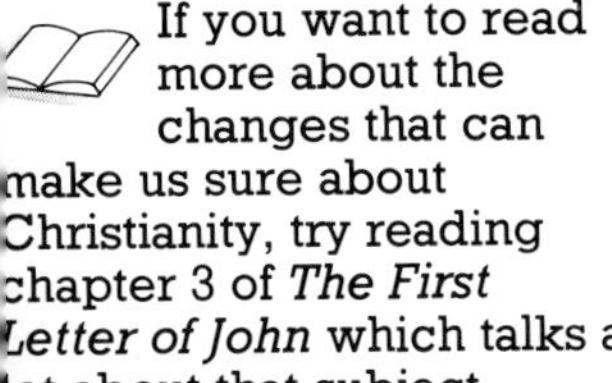

If you want to read more about the changes that can make us sure about Christianity, try reading chapter 3 of *The First Letter of John* which talks a lot about that subject.

No factsheet this week, but if you haven't read it yet, you can still have a copy of the booklet which explains how you can be sure of what you believe. Fill in the space on the **Reply card**.

Make a list of all the most important things you believe in. Then try to work out why you believe those things. Why are you sure about them?

Some of you may want to dig deeper into the evidence for Christianity. Some books which will help are:

The Day Death Died by Michael Green, which shows how you can be certain Jesus really did rise from death.

Belief by David Hewetson, which shows why it makes sense to believe the claims Jesus made.

Sure Thing by John Allan, which talks about five ways of proving to yourself that Christianity is true.

If stories are more your line, *Hell's Angel* by Brian Greenaway and Brian Kellock is the true story of how a tough biker, in prison for attempted murder, found he could be born again.

Fill in the space on the **Reply card** to get any of these books, or others like them.

OVER TO YOU

What do you think of Christianity now?

I THINK THAT . . .

- ☐ There is a good chance Christianity is true, but I can't be sure.
- ☐ It looks as if it **may** be possible to know for sure whether it's all true.
- ☐ Christianity is wishful thinking, with no good evidence behind it.
- ☐ I'm still not certain because

____

____

____

AND SO . . .

- ☐ I'll look at the evidence, then decide one way or the other.
- ☐ I'll invite God to give me a new life now, and then I'll know for sure.
- ☐ I'm not sure what I ought to do. I'll keep thinking.
- ☐ I'd like to _______________

____

____

____

SESSION

4

BEING A CHRISTIAN WHAT'S IT LIKE?

STARTER

WHICH ONE? Fill in your answers to the leader's questions here.

At home: A, B, or C?

On the road: G, H, or I?

At the party: P, Q, or R?

In the cinema queue: I, J, or K?

At the check-out: S, T, or U?

In scho S, T, or

BIBLE DATA

ɔw does a Christian approach life? To find one possible answer we'll look at Matthew 5.11 – 16:

11"Happy are you when people insult you
ıd persecute you and tell all kinds of evil
ɛs against you because you are my
llowers. 12Be happy and glad, for a great
ward is kept for you in heaven. This is how
e prophets who lived before you were
ɜrsecuted.
13"You are like salt for all mankind. But if
ılt loses its saltiness, there is no way to
ake it salty again. It has become worthless,
so it is thrown out and people trample on it.
14"You are like light for the whole world. A
city built on a hill cannot be hidden. 15No one
lights a lamp and puts it under a bowl;
instead he puts it on the lampstand, where it
gives light for everyone in the house. 16In the
same way your light must shine before
people, so that they will see the good things
you do and praise your Father in heaven . . ."
(Matthew 5.11–16)

ʒACKGROUND

This passage is part of the ɜmous "Sermon on the Mount", ı which Jesus spelled out clearly ʋhat he expected from his ɔllowers. You can read the whole ɦing in Matthew chapters 5–7.

• The main use of salt in Jesus' ɪome country was to preserve ɦeat — to prevent it going off. So ɜalt was essential for healthy ving — essential to keep lisease away.

ASK YOURSELVES...

? What effect does one person's behaviour have on those around?

REACTIONS

1 **Are there any things you don't understand about this passage, and would like explained?**

2 **Which, if any, of the following statements express what the passage says? If you wish, make up your own statement to explain what the passage says.**

If you're a Christian everyone will respect you for what you believe

Life here will be miserable, but heaven will make up for it all.

Christians should try to make people hate them, then they'll be happy.

Are any of these statements true? Why?

3 **Why did Jesus say Christians were to be like salt? How could a Christian be like salt in your home town?**

4 **What does it mean to let your light shine before people? How could a Christian do that in your town?**

5 **Have you met any Christians who have put you off, because they're like tasteless salt or because they're trying to keep their light out of sight? Share your experiences.**

Is there anything else in this passage which you want to discuss before moving on?

BACK-UP DATA

- How does a Christian feel about racial and sexual equality? See what Paul says in Galatians 3.26–29.
- What goes on in a Christian's mind? See, for example, Philippians 4.4–9.
- How does a Christian treat others? See one description in Colossians 3.12–17.

FACT-FILE

■ How did the first Christians affect others?

When Christianity arrived, the Roman world didn't know what had hit it! The great historian W.E.H. Lecky called it "a movement of philanthropy which has never been paralleled or approached in the pagan world". No wonder! Christians raised funds for the needy, began hospitals, cared for prison inmates, campaigned for the end of infant killing, campaigned for the humane treatment of slaves, supplied money to the unemployed, demonstrated against the cruelty of the Roman games — some record!

"You are like light for the whole world . . ." Matthew 5.14

■ Is Christianity boring?

Many people associate Christianity with out-of-date hymns and stuffy Gothic churches. But not everybody's into bring-and-buy sales! Each year there's a major Christian rock festival in Britain called Greenbelt, which attracts something like 30,000 people. Every Easter 10,000 Christians take over a holiday camp in Wales and have fun together as they worship God and learn a bit more from the Bible. There are Christian drama groups, dance teams, sports outfits, mountain-climbing centres . . . boring? Only if you're tired of living!

■ How do Christians respond to opposition?

Persecution has never daunted real Christians. The *World Christian Encyclopaedia* did fourteen years of research to find out how many Christians there are. It found that in the USSR, where Christians are often arrested and jailed, and non-Christian propaganda has been taught for over sixty years, there are still ninety-seven million Christians! In communist China there are over thirty million Christians, according to research agencies based in Hong Kong.

TAKE IT FURTHER

If you want to read more about the new life Christians can ive, and the Holy Spirit who makes it happen, read Galatians chapter 5. Note that "circumcision" is a physical operation which Jewish boys were supposed to have when they were babies. Some people were claiming that Christians had to have the operation in order to be real Christians. This chapter says, "No — that's not what counts".

Your leader can provide a helpful booklet which contains the basic advice new Christians need to help them. Fill in the space on the **Reply card** to get a copy.

Choose one problem area in your community — for example, unemployment; old people who live alone. Find out what Christians are doing to be "salt" and "light" in that area. Are there things they could do that they're not doing?

OVER TO YOU

This section is
FOR YOUR EYES ONLY
you don't have to show it to anyone else! But you can if you wish.

I THINK THAT . . .

- ☐ The ideals of Christianity are all right, but nobody can live up to them.
- ☐ It's possible to live a new, fulfilling, useful life with the Holy Spirit's power.
- ☐ Christianity's plan for living is naive, and way out of date.
- ☐ I'm still not certain because

____

____

____

____

AND SO . . .

- ☐ I'll suspend my judgment for one more week.
- ☐ I'll give up on Christianity and look for another way of living.
- ☐ I'll invite the Holy Spirit to start changing me and fulfilling my life.
- ☐ I'd like to ____________________

____

____

____

____

Remember that although your decision is completely your own, you can ask for advice or have a chat about things at any time you wish. You've only to say so on your **Reply card**, or approach your leader personally.

NEXT TIME

See you then.

STARTER

Well done! You've come to the last session. We'd just like to say: THANKS for giving up the time to come **Just Looking**. We hope you've enjoyed it and learnt a lot. We've appreciated your company.

Now a question. How many uses can you think of for a polystyrene cup? You're about to find out a few you had not thought of in "The great polystyrene cup massacre".

BIBLE DATA

What is the Church supposed to be for? Let's explore one way of looking at it in Colossians 1.24–29.

Paul's Work as a Servant of the Church

24 And now I am happy about my sufferings
for you, for by means of my physical
sufferings I am helping to complete what still
remains of Christ's sufferings on behalf of his
body, the church. 25 And I have been made a
servant of the church by God, who gave me
this task to perform for your good. It is the
task of fully proclaiming his message, 26 which
is the secret he hid through all past ages
from all mankind but has now revealed to his
people. 27 God's plan is to make known his
secret to his people, this rich and glorious
secret which he has for all peoples. And the
secret is that Christ is in you, which means
that you will share in the glory of God. 28 So
we preach Christ to everyone. With all
possible wisdom we warn and teach them in
order to bring each one into God's presence
as a mature individual in union with Christ.
29 To get this done I toil and struggle, using
the mighty strength which Christ supplies and
which is at work in me.
(Colossians 1.24–29)

REACTIONS

Are there any things you don't understand about this passage, and would like explained?

What is the secret that God wants all Christians to understand? Can you put it in your own words?

This is the way the secret is supposed to be made known:

How will "all people" get to hear and understand the secret?

Paul didn't just preach in order to get people born again! He wanted something more than that to happen to them. What was it?

So what is the Church for? According to this passage which of the following activities would be most likely to help it achieve that aim?

- ☐ *A save-the-steeple fund*
- ☐ *Teaching about what Christianity is*
- ☐ *Bingo in the church*
- ☐ *Ambitious plans to spread the message*
- ☐ *Regular prayer for the world*
- ☐ *Poetry readings and organ recitals*
- ☐ *Help for the oppressed*
- ☐ *(other)* ________
- ☐ *(other)* ________

Is there anything else in this passage which you want to discuss before moving on?

BACKGROUND

- These words were part of a letter sent by the Apostle Paul to one of the first Christian churches.
- Paul was a preacher, thinker, planner, and organizer — but first and foremost he saw himself as a "servant of the church".
- The people he was writing to had many problems: they had many wrong ideas, and some were living unchristian lives. But he didn't give up on them. They were still the Church, the family of God!

BACK-UP DATA

• How could wealthy churches use their money? See one example in 2 Corinthians 8.1–15.
• Does God expect churches to be full of middle-class people in fancy clothes, or should a church be broader than that? See what one writer has to say about it in James 2.1–4.
• Is it enough for church people to get together for an hour on a Sunday morning? See how Christianity is obviously much more than that in 1 Peter 4.7–11.

FACT-FILE

■ What about denominations?

There are 21,000 different denominations in the Church, and to some people that's a big problem. How can you talk about Christian love when there are so many competing varieties? But real Christians will get together regardless of denomination, and most of the big Christian organizations — for example Scripture Union, Bible Society, and Christian Aid, involve people from lots of different groups. They may prefer worshipping in different ways, but they still respect and work with one another.

■ Did the Church cause the war in Northern Ireland?

People will use any excuse when they want to cause trouble, and "religion" just happened to be the excuse in Ireland. It isn't the real Christians who are fighting. There are lots of Christian groups working for peace and reconciliation, and in some churches there are ex-IRA and UDA terrorists who have been "born again" and now have thrown away their Armalite rifles.

■ Is the Church too interested in money?

Sadly, sometimes it has been. There's no way you can defend the massive wealth some groups have accumulated, or the appeals for money some preachers make.

But, again, *real* Christians try to live simply and keep Jesus' attitude towards money. Some of the great relief movements were begun by poor Christians who trusted God. Last century George Muller opened orphanages all over the south-west of England — and he didn't have any money to his name. Lord Shaftesbury, founder of the Shaftesbury Society, nearly bankrupted himself trying to pay his servants what he thought was a fair wage.

TAKE IT FURTHER

If you want to read more about the way the Church is supposed to operate, and the way the Holy Spirit makes Christians fit in with each other, have a go at reading 1 Corinthians chapters 12 and 13.

If you want to know how you can go to church and actually enjoy it, there's a **Factsheet** called "How to go to church . . . and like it" which you can ask for when you fill in the **Reply card.**

Well, from here on in, it's up to you to decide how involved you want to get. Even if you're still not convinced about Christianity, keep going to church. Watch your Christian friends closely and see if they ring true. Read a passage of the Bible every day and ask God to speak to you through it. I believe he will, if you're prepared to listen to what he tells you!

OVER TO YOU

What's your conclusion? Read this part carefully. No boxes to tick, but one important decision to make.

If Christianity is true . . .
You can have a new life, "born again" into God's family. You can know for sure that it is true by the changes God makes in your life. You can start a lifelong friendship with Jesus Christ. You can experience all the power of the Holy Spirit making you "salt" and "light" in your world, helping people in need, fighting for justice and peace, finding real fulfilment as never before. You can become part of a new caring, trusting community. And most important, you're now God's friend. Your failures are forgiven. You're on your way to heaven.

If Christianity is not true . . .
You've just been studying the greatest hoax in the history of the world, and if you were conned by it you'd be living in a fool's paradise for the rest of your life. This world is probably meaningless, and you are just a temporary biological accident, doomed to extinction in a few years. If you don't like it, tough. What you have now is all you're going to get.

How will you ever know for sure if it's true, unless you give God a chance to do what he promises?

Does it make sense to reject what you've heard, without putting it to the test?

Can you find another philosophy which offers half so much personal satisfaction and challenge?

Other Beginnings books

Big Questions — by Rob Frost — "When I was a teenager I found myself asking some pretty basic questions. Questions about the purpose of life, the state of the world, and the existence of God. I was fortunate enough to belong to a youth group that gave me plenty of scope to think and talk. It was through this process that I began to turn to the Bible for answers, and eventually found Christ. My hope is that this book may help others to find him in the same way."

Conversation Starters — by Rob Frost — ". . . is for new Christians with a thousand questions on their minds. It's for new believers who are coming to terms with the Christian life. It's for new disciples who are trying to explain their experience to an unbelieving world."

Getting Going — by David Butterfield — Want to read the Bible but have lots of questions? "Who wrote it?" "Why is it so difficult to understand?" This book helps you explore the Bible on your own or as a group, and answers those questions at the same time.

On the Road — by Christopher Herbert — Bible studies to help you prepare for confirmation and church membership.

Stepping Out — by Frank Rinaldi — Interested in believer's baptism? Then this book is for you, whether you are getting ready to be baptized, or wanting to be reminded again of its meaning.

Go for Growth — by Rob Frost — If you want to grow as a Christian then *Go for Growth* is for you. It contains six exciting Bible study sessions on Paul's Letter to the Philippians. Subjects include: Why is Paul writing to the people in Philippi? Why do we need to grow as Christians? How do we serve others? What are our Christian attitudes?

New Discoveries — by John Allan — From the same author as *Just Looking* comes this fascinating new book that unlocks the secret of relevant Bible study. Six group sessions take you touring the world of the Bible. They show you how you can make your own discoveries. There are also five solo projects, called solo-flights, that will help you to use concordances and chain-references, and to study characters and key words.

your chance to believe it — or not

Reaction sheet

Now we've reached the end of **Just Looking,** we'd be grateful for some comments from you about how you found it. This will help us improve it for others in future! Fill in this questionnaire and give it to your group leader.

- What were the best things about **Just Looking?** ....
....
....
....

- What were the worst things? ....
....
....
....

- Have you any suggestions for possible improvements? ....
....
....
....

- How would you describe the effect it's had on you?
  - ☐ There's no change in my attitude.
  - ☐ I'm more interested in Christianity.
  - ☐ I've decided firmly against Christianity.
  - ☐ I've become a Christian.
  - ☐ I want to become a Christian.

- What was the most important thing you learned? ....
....
....
....

- Were there any other things you'd have liked to know about which we didn't deal with? ....
....
....
....

- Would you recommend the course to other people?
  - ☐ Yes.
  - ☐ No.
  - ☐ Not sure.

- Name and address (if you wish)..............
....
....
....

New Life
A new edition of the *Good News Bible*, including 80 full-colour pages. It explores what the Bible is, and how to use it. This is what some Christian leaders have to say about it:

New Life
"An ideal resource for today's Bible readers. At last here is the Bible made approachable."

— Rob Frost — *Author of three popular Beginnings books*

New Life
"Has special notes and guidelines to open up the text . . . I wholeheartedly recommend *New Life* to all who really want to read God's word regularly and act on what it says."

— Clive Calver — *General Secretary of the Evangelical Alliance*

New Life
". . . So readable with its helpful background notes and reading plans . . . they explore the whole Bible and yet continually focus on Jesus."

— Paul Montacute — *Baptist National Youth Officer*

New Life
"The Bible is always current and relevant. But sometimes it's not easy to understand. I know I'd have found this book helpful when I first decided to look at the Bible seriously."

— Cliff Richard — *International singer*

New Life
"What makes New Life so exceptional is its readers' guide which will encourage a realistic approach . . . young people and those working with them will find this Bible invaluable."

— David Isaac — *Anglican National Youth Officer*

If you would like to know more about this Bible, please tick here ☐